A Narrative of the Life and Adventures of Venture

A Narrative of the Life and Adventures of Venture

PREPARED FOR PUBLICATION

BY

HISTORIC PUBLISHING

All Rights Reserved. No part of this revised and edited publication may be reproduced, stored in a retrieval system, or transmitted, in any form, or by any means, electronic, mechanical, photocopying, recording, or otherwise, without the prior consent of the publisher.

HISTORIC PUBLISHING
©2017 (Edited Materials)

ISBN: 978-1946640222

A Narrative of the Life and Adventures of Venture

A Narrative of the
Life and Adventures of
Venture

A Native of Africa,
But Resident Above Sixty Years in the United
States of America.
Related by Himself.
By
Venture Smith
Edited
By
H. M. Selden

New London: First Printed in 1798.
Reprinted A. D. 1835, and Published by a
Descendant of Venture.
Revised and Republished with Traditions by
H. M. Selden, Haddam, Conn., 1896.
THIRD EDITION

MIDDLETOWN, CONN.:
J. S. STEWART, PRINTER AND
BOOKBINDER.
1897.

A Narrative of the Life and Adventures of Venture

A NARRATIVE --OF THE-- LIFE AND ADVENTURES --OF-- VENTURE A NATIVE OF AFRICA, But Resident Above Sixty Years in the United States of America. RELATED BY HIMSELF.

New London: Printed in 1798. Reprinted A. D. 1835, and Published by a Descendant of Venture.
Revised and Republished with Traditions by H. M. SELDEN, Haddam, Conn., 1896.

THIRD EDITION
LARGE PRINT EDITION

MIDDLETOWN, CONN.:
J. S. STEWART, PRINTER AND BOOKBINDER.
1897.

Entered according to Act of Congress in the year 1897, by HENRY M. SELDEN, in the Office of the Librarian of Congress, at Washington, D. C.

CONTENTS

PREFACE.   10
CHAPTER I.   15
CHAPTER II.   39
CHAPTER III.   70
CERTIFICATE.   93

TRADITIONS OF VENTURE! KNOWN AS VENTURE SMITH.   96

CHILDREN OF VENTURE AND MARGRET SMITH.   114

A Narrative of the Life and Adventures of Venture

PREFACE.

THE following account of the life of VENTURE is a relation of simple facts, in which nothing is added in substance to what he related himself. Many other interesting and curious passages of his life might have been inserted, but on account of the bulk to which they must necessarily have swelled this narrative, they were omitted. If any should suspect the truth of what is here related, they are referred to people now living who are acquainted with most of the facts mentioned in the narrative.

The reader is here presented with an account, not of a renowned politician or warrior, but of an untutored slave, brought into this Christian country at eight years of age, wholly destitute of all education but what he received in common with domesticated animals, enjoying no advantages that could lead him to suppose himself superior to the beasts, his fellow-servants. And, if he shall derive no other advantage from perusing this narrative, he may experience those sensations of shame and indignation that will prove him to be not wholly destitute of every noble and generous feeling.

The subject of the following pages, had he received only a common education, might have been a man of high respectability and usefulness; and had his education been suited to his genius, he might have been an ornament and an honor to human nature. It may, perhaps, not be unpleasing to see the efforts of a great mind wholly uncultivated, enfeebled and depressed by slavery, and struggling under every disadvantage. The reader may here see a Franklin and a Washington, in a state of nature, or, rather, in a state of slavery. Destitute as he is of all education, and broken by hardships and infirmities of age, he still exhibits striking traces of native ingenuity and good sense.

This narrative exhibits a pattern of honesty, prudence and industry to people of his own color; and perhaps some white people would not find themselves degraded by imitating such an example.

The following account is published in compliance with the earnest desire of the subject of it, and likewise a number of respectable persons who are acquainted with him.

A Narrative of the Life and Adventures of Venture

NARRATIVE OF LIFE OF VENTURE.

CHAPTER I.

CONTAINING AN ACCOUNT OF HIS LIFE, FROM HIS BIRTH TO THE TIME OF HIS LEAVING HIS NATIVE COUNTRY.

I WAS born at Dukandarra, in Guinea, about the year 1729. My father's name was Saungm Furro, Prince of the tribe of Dukandarra. My father had three wives. Polygamy was not uncommon in that country, especially among the rich, as every man was allowed to keep as many wives as he could maintain. By his first wife he had three children. The eldest of them was myself, named by my father, Broteer. The other two were named Cundazo and

Soozaduka. My father had two children by his second wife, and one by his third. I descended from a very large, tall and stout race of beings, much larger than the generality of people in other parts of the globe, being commonly considerable above six feet in height, and every way well proportioned.

The first thing worthy of notice which I remember, was a contention between my father and mother, on account of my father marrying his third wife without the consent of his first and eldest, which was contrary to the custom generally observed among my countrymen. In consequence of this rupture, my mother left her husband and country, and travelled away with her three children to the eastward. I was then five years old. She took not the least sustenance along with her, to support either herself or children. I was able to travel along by her side; the other two of her offspring she carried, one on her back, the other, being a sucking child, in her arms. When we became hungry, our mother used to set us down on the ground and gather some of the fruits that grew spontaneously in that climate. These served us for food on the way. At night we all lay down together in the most secure place we could find and reposed ourselves until morning. Though there were many noxious animals there, yet so kind was our Almighty protector that none of them were ever permitted to hurt or molest us.

Thus, we went on our journey until the second day after our departure from Dukandarra, when we came to the entrance of a great desert. During our travel in that, we were often affrighted with the doleful howlings and yelling's of wolves, lions and other animals. After five days travel, we came to the end of this desert, and immediately entered into a beautiful and extensive interval country. Here my mother was pleased to stop and seek a refuge for me. She left me at the house of a very rich farmer. I was then, as I should judge, not less than one hundred and forty miles from my native place, separated from all my relatives and acquaintances. At this place, my mother took her farewell of me and set out for her own country. My new guardian, as I shall call the man with whom I was left, put me into the business of tending sheep immediately after I was left with him. The flock, which I kept with the assistance of a boy, consisted of about forty. We drove them every morning between two and three miles to pasture, into the wide and delightful plains. When night drew on, we drove them home and secured them in the cote. In this round I continued during my stay here. One incident which befel me when I was driving my flock from pasture, was so dreadful to me at that age, and is to this time so fresh in my memory, that I cannot help noticing it in this place. Two large dogs sallied out of a certain house and set upon me. One of them took me by the arm and the other by the thigh, and before their master could come and relieve me, they lacerated my flesh to such a degree that the scars are very visible to the present day. My master was immediately sent for. He came and carried me home, as I was unable to go myself on account of my wounds. Nothing remarkable happened afterwards until my father sent for me to return home.

Before I dismiss this country, I must first inform my reader what I remember concerning this place. A large river runs through this country in a westerly course. The land for a great way on each side is flat and level, hedged in by a considerable rise in the country at a great distance from it. It scarce ever rains there, yet the land is fertile; great dews fall in the night, which refresh the soil. About the latter end of June or first of July, the river begins to rise, and gradually increases until it has inundated the country for a great distance, to the height of seven or eight feet. This brings on a slime, which enriches the land surprisingly. When the river has subsided, the natives begin to sow and plant, and the vegetation is exceeding rapid. Near this rich river my guardian's land lay. He possessed, I cannot exactly tell how much, yet this I am certain of respecting it, that he owned an immense tract. He possessed likewise a great many cattle and goats. During my stay with him I was kindly used, and with as much tenderness, for what I saw, as his only son, although I was an entire stranger to him, remote from friends and relatives. The principal occupations of the inhabitants there were the cultivation of the soil and the care of their flocks. They were a people pretty similar in every respect to that of mine, except in their persons, which were not so tall and stout. They appeared to be very kind and friendly. I will now return to my departure from that place.

My father sent a man and horse after me. After settling with my guardian for keeping me, he took me away and went for home. It was then about one year since my mother brought me here. Nothing remarkable occurred to us on our journey until we arrived safe home. I found then that the difference between my parents had been made up previous to their sending for me. On my return, I was received both by my father and mother with great joy and affection, and was once more restored to my paternal dwelling in peace and happiness. I was then about six years old.

Not more than six weeks had passed after my return, before a message was brought by an inhabitant of the place where I lived the preceding year to my father, that that place had been invaded by a numerous army, from a nation not far distant, furnished with musical instruments, and all kinds of arms then in use; that they were instigated by some white nation who equipped and sent them to subdue and possess the country; that his nation had made no preparation for war, having been for a long time in profound peace; that they could not defend themselves against such a formidable train of invaders, and must, therefore, necessarily evacuate their lands to the fierce enemy, and fly to the protection of some chief; and that if he would permit them they would come under his rule and protection when they had to retreat from their own possessions. He was a kind and merciful prince, and therefore consented to these proposals.

He had scarcely returned to his nation with the message before the whole of his people were obliged to retreat from their country and come to my father's dominions. He gave them every privilege and all the protection his government could afford. But they had not been there longer than four days before news came to them that the invaders had laid waste their country, and were coming speedily to destroy them in my father's territories. This affrighted them, and therefore they immediately pushed off to the southward, into the unknown countries there, and were never more heard of.

Two days after their retreat, the report turned out to be but too true. A detachment from the enemy came to my father and informed him that the whole army was encamped not far from his dominions, and would invade the territory and deprive his people of their liberties and rights, if he did not comply with the following terms. These were, to pay them a large sum, of money, three hundred fat cattle, and a great number of goats, sheep, asses, etc.

My father told the messenger he would comply rather than that his subjects should be deprived of their rights and privileges, which he was not then in circumstances to defend from so sudden an invasion. Upon turning out those articles, the enemy pledged their faith and honor that they would not attack him. On these he relied, and therefore thought it unnecessary to be on his guard against the enemy. But their pledges of faith and honor proved no better than those of other unprincipled hostile nations, for a few days after, a certain relation of the king came and informed him that the enemy who sent terms of accommodation to him, and received tribute to their satisfaction, yet meditated an attack upon his subjects by surprise, and that probably they would commence their attack in less than one day, and concluded with advising him, as he was not prepared for war, to order a speedy retreat of his family and subjects. He complied with this advice.

The same night which was fixed upon to retreat, my father and his family set off about the break of day. The king and his two younger wives went in one company, and my mother and her children in another. We left our dwellings in succession, and my father's company went on first. We directed our course for a large shrub plain, some distance off, where we intended to conceal ourselves from the approaching enemy, until we could refresh ourselves a little. But we presently found that our retreat was not secure. For having struck up a little fire for the purpose of cooking victuals, the enemy, who happened to be encamped a little distance off, had sent out a scouting party who discovered us by the smoke of the fire, just as we were extinguishing it and about to eat. As soon as we had finished eating, my father discovered the party and immediately began to discharge arrows at them. This was what I first saw, and it alarmed both me and the women, who, being unable to make any resistance, immediately betook ourselves to the tall, thick reeds not far off, and left the old king to fight alone. For some time I beheld him from the reeds defending himself with great courage and firmness, till at last he was obliged to surrender himself into their hands.

    They then came to us in the reeds, and the very first salute I had from them was a violent blow on the head with the fore part of a gun, and at the same time a grasp round the neck. I then had a rope put about my neck, as had all the women in the thicket with me, and were immediately led to my father, who was likewise pinioned and haltered for leading. In this condition we were all led to the camp. The women and myself, being submissive, had tolerable treatment from the enemy, while my father was closely interrogated respecting his money, which they knew he must have. But as he gave them no account of it, he was instantly cut and pounded on his body with great inhumanity, that he might be induced by the torture he suffered to make the discovery. All this availed not in the least to make him give up his money, but he despised all the tortures which they inflicted, until the continued exercise and increase of torment obliged him to sink and expire. He thus died without informing his enemies where his money lay. I saw him while he was thus tortured to death. The shocking scene is to this day fresh in my memory, and I have often been overcome while thinking on it. He was a man of remarkable stature. I should judge as much as six feet and six or seven inches high, two feet across the shoulders, and every way well proportioned. He was a man of remarkable strength and resolution, affable, kind and gentle, ruling with equity and moderation.

The army of the enemy was large, I should suppose consisting of about six thousand men. Their leader was called Baukurre. After destroying the old prince, they decamped and immediately marched towards the sea, lying to the west, taking with them myself and the women prisoners. In the march, a scouting party was detached from the main army. To the leader of this party I was made waiter, having to carry his gun, etc. As we were a scouting, we came across a herd of fat cattle consisting of about thirty in number. These we set upon and immediately wrested from their keepers, and afterwards converted them into food for the army. The enemy had remarkable success in destroying the country wherever they went. For as far as they had penetrated they laid the habitations waste and captured the people. The distance they had now brought me was about four hundred miles. All the march I had very hard tasks imposed on me, which I must perform on pain of punishment. I was obliged to carry on my head a large flat stone used for grinding our corn, weighing, as I should suppose, as much as twenty-five pounds; besides victuals, mat and cooking utensils. Though I was pretty large and stout of my age, yet these burdens were very grievous to me, being only six years and a half old.

We were then come to a place called Malagasco. When we entered the place, we could not see the least appearance of either houses or inhabitants, but on stricter search found that instead of houses above ground they had dens in the sides of hillocks, contiguous to ponds and streams of water. In these we perceived they had all hid themselves, as I suppose they usually did on such occasions. In order to compel them to surrender, the enemy contrived to smoke them out with faggots. These they put to the entrance of the caves and set them on fire.

While they were engaged in this business, to their great surprise some of them were desperately wounded with arrows, which fell from above on them. This mystery they soon found out. They perceived that the enemy discharged these arrows through holes on the top of the dens directly into the air. Their weight brought them back, point downwards, on their enemies heads, whilst they were smoking the inhabitants out. The points of their arrows were poisoned, but their enemy had an antidote for it which they instantly applied to the wounded part. The smoke at last obliged the people to give themselves up. They came out of their caves, first spatting the palms of their hands together, and immediately after extended their arms, crossed at their wrists ready to be bound and pinioned. I should judge that the dens above mentioned were extended about eight feet horizontally into the earth, six feet in height, and as many wide. They were arched overhead and lined with earth, which was of the clay kind and made the surface of their walls firm and smooth.

The invaders then pinioned the prisoners of all ages and sexes indiscriminately, took their flocks and all their effects, and moved on their way towards the sea. On the march, the prisoners were treated with clemency, on account of their being submissive and humble. Having come to the next tribe, the enemy laid siege and immediately took men, women, children, flocks, and all their valuable effects. They then went on to the next district, which was contiguous to the sea, called in Africa, Anamaboo. The enemies' provisions were then almost spent, as well as their strength. The inhabitants, knowing what conduct they had pursued, and what were their present intentions, improved the favorable opportunity, attacked them, and took enemy, prisoners, flocks and all their effects. I was then taken a second time. All of us were then put into the castle and kept for market. On a certain time, I and other prisoners were put on board a canoe, under our master, and rowed away to a vessel belonging to Rhode Island, commanded by Captain Collingwood, and the mate, Thomas Mumford. While we were going to the vessel, our master told us to appear to the best possible advantage for sale. I was bought on board by one Robertson Mumford, steward of said vessel, for four gallons of rum and a piece of calico, and called VENTURE, on account of his having purchased me with his own private venture. Thus I came by my name. All the slaves that were bought for that vessel's cargo were two hundred and sixty.

CHAPTER II.

CONTAINING AN ACCOUNT OF HIS LIFE FROM THE TIME OF HIS LEAVING AFRICA TO THAT OF HIS BECOMING FREE.

AFTER all the business was ended on the coast of Africa, the ship sailed from thence to Barbadoes. After an ordinary passage, except great mortality by the small pox, which broke out on board, we arrived at the island of Barbadoes; but when we reached it, there were found, out of the two hundred and sixty that sailed from Africa, not more than two hundred alive. These were all sold, except myself and three more, to the planters there.

The vessel then sailed for Rhode Island, and arrived there after a comfortable passage. Here my master sent me to live with one of his sisters until he could carry me to Fisher's Island, the place of his residence. I had then completed my eighth year. After staying with his sister some time, I was taken to my master's place to live.

When we arrived at Narraganset, my master went ashore in order to return a part of the way by land, and gave me the charge of the keys of his trunks on board of the vessel, and charged me not to deliver them up to anybody, not even to his father, without his orders. To his directions I promised faithfully to conform. When I arrived with my master's articles at his house, my master's father asked me for his son's keys, as he wanted to see what his trunks contained. I told him that my master intrusted me with the care of them until he should return, and that I had given him my word to be faithful to the trust, and could not, therefore, give him, or any other man, the keys without my master's directions. He insisted that I should deliver to him the keys on pain of punishment. But I let him know that he should not have them, let him say what he would. He then laid aside trying to get them. But notwithstanding he appeared to give up trying to obtain them from me, yet I mistrusted that he would take some time when I was off my guard, either in the daytime or at night, to get them, therefore, I slung them round my neck, and in the daytime concealed them in my bosom, and at night I always slept with them under me, that no person might take them from me without my being apprised of it. Thus I kept the keys from everybody until my master came home. When he returned he asked where VENTURE was. As I was within hearing, I came and said, "Here, sir, at your service." He asked for his keys, and I immediately took them off my neck and reached them out to him. He took them, stroked my hair, and commended me, saying in presence of his father that his young VENTURE was so faithful that he never would have been able to have taken the keys from him but by violence; that he should not fear to trust him with his whole fortune, for that he had been in his native place so habituated to keeping his word, that he would sacrifice even his life to maintain it.

The first of the time of living at my master's own place, I was pretty much employed in the house, carding wool and other household business. In this situation I continued for some years, after which my master put me to work out of doors. After, many proofs of my faithfulness and honesty, my master began to put great confidence in me. My behavior had as yet been submissive and obedient. I then began to have hard tasks imposed on me. Some of these were to pound four bushels of ears of corn every night in a barrel for the poultry, or be rigorously punished. At other seasons of the year, I had to card wool until a very late hour. These tasks I had to perform when only about nine years old. Sometime after, I had another difficulty and oppression which was greater than any I had ever experienced since I came into this country. This was to serve two masters. James Mumford, my master's son, when his father had gone from home in the morning and given me a stint to perform that day, would order me to do this and that business different from what my master had directed me. One day in particular, the authority which my master's son had set up had like to have produced melancholy effects. For my master having set me off my business to perform that day and then left me to perform it, his son came up to me in the course of the day, big with authority, and commanded me very arrogantly to quit my present business and go directly about what he should order me. I replied to him that my master had given. me so much to perform that day, and that I must faithfully complete it in that time. He then broke out into a great rage, snatched a pitchfork and went to lay me over the head therewith, but I as soon got another and defended myself with it, or otherwise he might have murdered me in his outrage. He immediately called some people who were within hearing at work for him, and ordered them to take his hair rope and come and bind me with it. They all tried to bind me, but in vain, though there were three assistants in number. My upstart master then desisted, put his pocket handkerchief before his eyes and went home with a design to tell his mother of the struggle with young VENTURE. He told that their young VENTURE had become so stubborn that he could not control him, and asked her what he should do with him. In the meantime I recovered my temper, voluntarily caused myself to be bound by the same men who tried in vain before, and carried before my young master, that he might do what he pleased with me. He took me to a gallows made for the purpose of hanging cattle on, and suspended me on it. Afterwards he ordered one of his hands to go to the peach orchard and cut him three dozen of whips to punish me with. These were brought to him, and that was all that was done with them, as I was released and went to work after hanging on the gallows about an hour.

After I had lived with my master thirteen years, being then about twenty-two years old, I married Meg, a slave of his who was about my own age. My master owned a certain Irishman, named Heddy, who about that time formed a plan of secretly leaving his master. After he had long had this plan in meditation, he suggested it to me. At first I cast a deaf-ear to it, and rebuked Heddy for harboring in his mind such a rash undertaking. But after he had persuaded and much enchanted me with the prospect of gaining my freedom by such a method, I at length agreed to accompany him. Heddy next inveigled two of his fellow-servants to accompany us. The place to which we designed to go was the Mississippi. Our next business was to lay in a sufficient store of provisions for our voyage. We privately collected out of our master's store, six great old cheeses, two firkins of butter, and one batch of new bread. When we had gathered all our own clothes and some more, we took them all about midnight and went to the water side. We stole our master's boat, embarked, and then directed our course for the Mississippi River.

We mutually confederated not to betray or desert one another on pain of death. We first steered our course for Montauk Point, the east end of Long Island. After our arrival there, we landed, and Heddy and I made an incursion into the island after fresh water, while our two comrades were left a little distance from the boat, employed in cooking. When Heddy and I had sought some time for water, he returned to our companions and I continued on looking for my object. When Heddy had performed his business with our companions who were engaged in cooking, he went directly to the boat, stole all the clothes in it, and then travelled away for East Hampton, as I was informed. I returned to my fellows not long after. They informed me that our clothes were stolen, but could not determine who was the thief, yet they suspected Heddy, as he was missing. After reproving my comrades for not taking care of our things which were in the boat, I advertised Heddy and sent two men in search of him. They pursued and overtook him at Southampton and returned him to the boat. I then thought it might afford some chance for my freedom, or at least be a palliation for my running away, to return Heddy immediately to his master, and inform him that I was induced to go away by Heddy's address. Accordingly, I set off with him and the rest of my companions for my master's, and arrived there without any difficulty. I informed my master that Heddy was the ringleader of our revolt, and that he had used us ill. He immediately put Heddy into custody, and myself and companions were well received and went to work as usual.

Not a long time passed after that before Heddy was sent by my master to New London gaol. At the close of that year I was sold to a Thomas Stanton, and had to be separated from my wife and one daughter, who was about one month old. He resided at Stonington Point. To this place I brought with me from my late master's, two Johannes, three old Spanish dollars, and two thousand of coppers, besides five pounds of my wife's money. This money I got by cleaning gentlemen's shoes and drawing-boots, by catching muskrats and minks, raising potatoes and carrots, etc., and by fishing in the night, and at odd spells.

All this money, amounting to near twenty-one pounds York currency, my master's brother, Robert Stanton, hired of me, for which he gave me his note. About a year and a half after that time, my master purchased my wife and her child for seven hundred pounds old tenor. One time my master sent me two miles after a barrel of molasses, and ordered me to carry it on my shoulders. I made out to carry it all the way to my master's house. When I lived with Capt. George Mumford, only to try my strength I took upon my knees a tierce of salt containing seven bushels, and carried it two or three rods. Of this fact there are several eye witnesses now living.

Towards the close of the time that I resided with this master, I had a falling out with my mistress. This happened one time when my master was gone to Long Island a-gunning. At first the quarrel began between my wife and her mistress. I was then at work in the barn, and hearing a racket in the house, induced me to run there and see what had broken out. When I entered the house, I found my mistress in a violent passion with my wife, for what she informed me was a mere trifle--such a small affair that I forbear to put my mistress to the shame of having it known.

I earnestly requested my wife to beg pardon of her mistress for the sake of peace, even if she had given no just occasion for offence. But whilst I was thus saying, my mistress turned the blows which she was repeating on my wife to me. She took down her horse whip, and while she was glutting her fury with it, I reached out my great black hand, raised it up and received the blows of the whip on it which were designed for my head. Then I immediately committed the whip to the devouring fire.

When my master returned from the island, his wife told him of the affair, but for the present he seemed to take no notice of it, and mentioned not a word of it to me. Some days after his return, in the morning as I was putting on a log in the fire-place, not suspecting harm from any one, I received a most violent stroke on the crown of my head with a club two feet long and as large around as a chair post. This blow very badly wounded my head, and the scar of it remains to this day. The first blow made me have my wits about me you may suppose, for as soon as he went to renew it I snatched the club out of his hands and dragged him out of the door. He then sent for his brother to come and assist him, but I presently left my master, took the club he wounded me with carried it to a neighboring justice of the peace, and complained of my master. He finally advised me to return to my master and live contented with him till he abused me again, and then complain. I consented to do accordingly. But before I set out for my master's, up he came and his brother Robert after me. The justice improved this convenient opportunity to caution my master. He asked him for what he treated his slave thus hastily and unjustly, and told him what would be the consequence if he continued the same treatment towards me. After the justice had ended his discourse with my master, he and his brother set out with me for home, one before and the other behind me. When they had come to a by-place, they both dismounted their respective horses and fell to beating me with great violence. I became enraged at this and immediately turned them both under me, laid one of them across the other, and stamped them both with my feet what I would.

This occasioned my master's brother to advise him to put me off. A short time after this, I was taken by a constable and two men. They carried me to a blacksmith's shop and had me handcuffed. When I returned home my mistress enquired much of her waiters whether VENTURE was handcuffed. When she was informed that I was, she appeared to be very contented and was much transported with the news. In the midst of this content and joy, I presented myself before my mistress, showed her my handcuffs, and gave her thanks for my gold rings. For this my master commanded a negro of his to fetch him a large ox chain. This my master locked on my legs with two padlocks. I continued to wear the chain peaceably for two or three days, when my master asked me with contempuous hard names whether I had not better be freed from my chains and go to work. I answered him, "No." "Well, then," said he, "I will send you to the West Indies, or banish you, for I am resolved not to keep you." I answered him, "I crossed the waters to come here and I am willing to cross them to return."

For a day or two after this not anyone said much to me, until one Hempstead Miner of Stonington asked me if I would live with him. I answered that I would. He then requested me to make myself discontented and to appear as unreconciled to my master as I could before that he bargained with him for me, and that in return he would give me a good chance to gain my freedom when I came to live with him. I did as he requested me. Not long after, Hempstead Miner purchased me of my master for fifty-six pounds lawful. He took the chain and padlocks from off me immediately after.

It may here be remembered that I related a few pages back that I hired out a sum of money to Mr. Robert Stanton, and took his note for it. In the fray between my master Stanton and myself, he broke open my chest containing his brother's note to me and destroyed it. Immediately after my present master bought me, he determined to sell me at Hartford. As soon as I became apprised of it, I bethought myself that I would secure a certain sum of money which lay by me safer than to hire it out to Stanton. Accordingly I buried it in the earth, a little distance from Thomas Stanton's, in the road over which he passed daily. A short time after, my master carried me to Hartford, and first proposed to sell me to one William Hooker of that place. Hooker asked whether I would go to the German Flats with him. I answered, "No." He said I should; if not by fair means, I should by foul. "If you will go by no other measures, I will tie you down in my sleigh." I replied to him, that if he carried me in that manner no person would purchase me, for it would be thought he had a murderer for sale. After this he tried no more, and said he would not have me as a gift.

My master next offered me to Daniel Edwards, Esq., of Hartford, for sale. But he not purchasing me, my master pawned me to him for ten pounds, and returned to Stonington. After some trial of my honesty, Mr. Edwards placed considerable trust and confidence in me. He put me to, serve as his cupbearer and waiter. When there was company at his house, he would send me into his cellar and other parts of his house to fetch wine and other articles occasionally for them. When I had been with him some time, he asked me why my master wished to part with such an honest negro, and why he did not keep me himself. I replied that I could not give him the reason, unless it was to convert me into cash and speculate with me as with other commodities. I hope that he can never justly say it was on account of my ill conduct that he did not keep me himself. Mr. Edwards told me that he should be very willing to keep me himself, and that he would never let me go from him to live, if it was not unreasonable and inconvenient for me to be parted from my wife and children; therefore, he would furnish me with a horse to return to Stonington, if I had a mind, for it. As Miner did not appear to redeem me, I went, and called at my old master Stanton's first to see my wife, who was then owned by him. As my old master appeared much ruffled at my being there, I left my wife before I had spent any considerable time with her, and went to Col. O. Smith's. Miner had not as yet wholly settled with Stanton for me, and had before my return from Hartford given Colonel Smith a bill of sale of me. These men once met to determine which of them should hold me, and upon my expressing a desire to be owned by Colonel Smith, and upon my master's settling the remainder of the money which was due to Stanton for me, it was agreed that I should live with Colonel

Smith. This was the third time of my being sold, and I was then thirty-one years old.

As I never had an opportunity of redeeming myself whilst I was owned by Miner, though he promised to give me a chance, I was then very ambitious of obtaining it. I asked my master one time if he would consent to have me purchase my freedom. He replied that he would. I was then very happy, knowing that I was at that time able to pay part of the purchase money by means of the money which I some time buried. This I took out of the earth and tendered to my master, having previously engaged a free negro man to take his security for it, as I was the property of my master, and therefore could not safely take his obligation myself. What was wanting in redeeming myself, my master agreed to wait on me for, until I could procure it for him. I still continued to work for Colonel Smith. There was continually some interest accruing on my master's note to my friend, the free negro man above named, which I received, and with some besides, which I got by fishing, I laid out in land adjoining my old master Stanton's. By cultivating this land with the greatest diligence and economy, at times when my master did not require my labor, in two years I laid up ten pounds. This my friend tendered my master for myself, and received his note for it.

Being encouraged by the success which I had met in redeeming myself, I again solicited my master for a further chance of completing it. The chance for which I solicited him was that of going out to work the ensuing winter. He agreed to this on condition that I would give him one-quarter of my earnings. On these terms I worked the following winter, and earned four pounds and sixteen shillings, one quarter of which went to my master for the privilege, and the rest was paid him on my account. I was then about thirty-five years old.

"The next summer I again desired he would give me a chance of going to work. But he refused and answered that he must have my labor this summer, as he did not have it the past winter. I replied that I considered it as hard that I could not have a chance to work out when the season become advantageous, and that I must only be permitted to hire myself out in the poorest season of the year. He asked me after this what I would give him for the privilege per month. I replied that I would leave it wholly to his own generosity to determine what I should return him a month. Well then, said he, if so, two pounds a month. I answered him that if that was the least he would take I would be contented.

    Accordingly I hired myself out at Fisher's Island, earning twenty pounds; thirteen pounds six shillings of which my master drew for the privilege and the remainder I paid for my freedom. This made fifty-one pounds two shillings which I paid him. In October following I went and wrought six months at Long Island. In that six months' time I cut and corded four hundred cords of wood, besides threshing out seventy-five bushels of grain, and received of my wages down only twenty pounds, which left remaining a larger sum. Whilst I was out that time, I took up on my wages only one pair of shoes. At night I lay on the hearth, with one coverlet over and another under me. I returned to my master and gave him what I received of my six months' labor. This left only thirteen pounds eighteen shillings-to-make up the full sum of my redemption. My master liberated me, saying that I might pay what was behind if I could ever make it convenient, otherwise it would be well. The amount of the money which I had paid my master towards redeeming my time, was seventy-one pounds two shillings. The reason of my master for asking such an unreasonable price, was, he said, to secure himself in case I should ever come to want. Being thirty-six years old, I left Colonel Smith once more for all. I had already been sold three different times, made considerable money with seemingly nothing to derive it from, had been cheated out of a large sum of money, lost much by misfortunes, and paid an enormous sum for my freedom.

CHAPTER III.

CONTAINING AN ACCOUNT OF HIS LIFE FROM THE TIME OF PURCHASING HIS FREEDOM TO THE PRESENT DAY.

MY wife and children were yet in bondage to Mr. Thomas Stanton. About this time I lost a chest containing, besides clothing, about thirty eight pounds in paper money. It was burnt by accident. A short time after I sold all my possessions at Stonington, consisting of a pretty piece of land and one dwelling house thereon, and went to reside at Long Island. For the first four years of my residence there, I spent my time in working for various people on that and at the neighboring islands. In the space of six months I cut and corded upwards of four hundred cords of wood. Many other singular and wonderful labors I performed in cutting wood there, which would not be inferior to the one just recited, but for brevity's sake I must omit them. In the aforementioned four years, what wood I cut at Long Island amounted to several thousand cords, and the money, which I earned thereby amounted to two hundred and seven pounds ten shillings. This money I laid up carefully by me. Perhaps some may inquire what maintained me all the time I was laying up my money. I would inform them that I bought nothing which I did not absolutely want. All fine clothes I despised in comparison with my interest, and never kept but just what clothes were comfortable for common days, and perhaps I would have a garment or two which I did not have on at all times, but as for superfluous finery. I never thought it to be compared with a decent homespun dress, a good supply of money and prudence. Expensive gatherings of my mates I commonly shunned, and all kinds of luxuries. I was perfectly a stranger to; and during the time I was employed in cutting the aforementioned quantity of wood, I never was at the expense of six pence worth of spirits. Being after this labor forty years of age, I worked at various places, and in particular on Ram Island, where I purchased Solomon and Cuff, two sons of mine, for two hundred dollars each.

It will here be remembered how much money I earned by cutting wood in four years. Besides this, I had considerable money, amounting to all to near three hundred pounds. After this I purchased a negro man, for no other reason than to oblige him, and gave for him sixty pounds. But in a short time after he ran away from me, and I thereby lost all that I gave for him, except twenty pounds which he paid me previous to his absconding. The rest of my money I laid out in land, in addition to a farm which I owned before, and a dwelling house thereon. Forty-four years had then completed their revolution since my entrance into this existence of servitude and misfortune.

Solomon, my eldest son, being then in his seventeenth year, and all my hope and dependence for help, I hired him out to one Charles Church, of Rhode Island, for one year, on consideration of his giving him twelve pounds and an opportunity of acquiring some learning. In the course of the year, Church fitted out a vessel for a whaling voyage, and being in want of hands to man her, he induced my son to go, with the promise of giving him on his return, a pair of silver buckles, besides his wages, As soon as I heard of his going to sea, I immediately set out to go and prevent it if possible. But on my arrival at Church's, to my great grief, I could only see the vessel my son was in, almost out of sight, going to sea. My son died of the scurvy in this voyage, and Church has never yet paid me the least of his wages. In my son, besides the loss of his life, I lost, equal to seventy-five pounds.

My other son being but a youth, still lived with me. About this time I chartered a sloop of about thirty tons burthen, and hired men to assist me in navigating her. I employed her mostly in the wood trade to Rhode Island, and made clear of all expenses above one hundred dollars with her in better than one year. I had then become something forehanded and being in my forth-fourth year, I purchased my wife Meg, and thereby prevented having another child to buy, as she was then pregnant. I gave forty pounds for her.

    During my residence at Long Island, I raised one year with another, ten cart loads of watermelons, and lost a great many besides by the thievishness of the sailors. What I made by the watermelons I sold there, amounted to nearly five hundred dollars. Various other methods. I pursued in order to enable me to redeem my family. In the night time I fished with set-nets and pots for eels and lobsters, and shortly after went a whaling voyage in the service of Col. Smith. After being out seven months, the vessel returned laden with four hundred barrels of oil. About this time I became possessed of another dwelling house, and my temporal affairs were in a pretty prosperous condition. This and my industry was what alone saved me from being expelled that part of the island in which I resided, as an act was passed by the selectmen of the place, that all negroes residing there should be expelled.

Next after my wife. I purchased a negro man for four hundred dollars. But he having an inclination to return to his old master, I therefore let him go. Shortly after, I purchased another negro man for twenty-five pounds, whom I parted with shortly after.

Being about forty-six years old, I bought my oldest child,

Hannah, of Ray Mumford, for forty-four pounds, and she still resided with him. I had already redeemed from slavery, myself, my wife and three children, besides three negro men.

About the forty-seventh year of my life I disposed of all my property at Long Island, and came from thence into East Haddam, Conn. I hired myself out first to Timothy Chapman for five weeks, the earnings of which time I put up carefully by me. After this I wrought for Abel Bingham for about six weeks. I then put my money together and purchased of said Bingham ten acres of land lying at Haddam Neck, where I now reside. On this land I labored with great diligence two years, and shortly after purchased six acres more of land contiguous to my other. One year from that time I purchased seventy acres more of the same man, and paid for it mostly with the produce of my other land. Soon after I bought this last lot of land, I set up a comfortable dwelling house on my farm, and built it from the produce thereof. Shortly after I had much trouble and expense with my daughter Hannah, whose name has been before mentioned to this account. She was soon married after I redeemed her, to one Isaac, and shortly after her marriage fell sick of a mortal disease Her husband, a dissolute and abandoned wretch, paid but little attention to her illness. I therefore thought it best to bring her to my house and nurse her there. I procured her all the aid mortals could afford, but notwithstanding this she fell a prey to her disease, after a lingering and painful endurance of it. The physician's bill for attending her illness amounted to forty pounds

Having reached my fifty-fourth year, I hired two negro men, one named William Jacklin, and the other, Mingo. Mingo lived with me one year, and having received his wages, run in debt to me eight dollars, for which he gave me his note. Presently after he tried to run away from me without troubling himself to pay up his note. I procured a warrant, took him, and requested him to go to

Justice Throop's of his own accord, but he refusing, I took him on my shoulders and carried him there, distant about two miles. The justice asking me if I had my prisoner's note with me, and replying that I had not, he told me that I must return with him and get it. Accordingly, I carried Mingo back on my shoulders, but before we arrived at my dwelling, he complained of being hurt, and asked me if this was not a hard way of treating our fellow-creatures. I answered him that it would be hard thus to treat our honest fellow-creatures. He then told me that if I would let him off my shoulders, he had a pair of silver shoe-buckles, one shirt and a pocket handkerchief, which he would turn out to me. I agreed, and let him return home with me on foot; but the very following night he slipped from me, stole my horse and has never paid me even his note. The other negro man, Jacklin, being a comb-maker by trade, he requested me to set him up, and promised to reward me well with his labor. Accordingly I bought him a set of tools for making combs, and procured him stock. He worked at my house about one year, and then ran away from me with all his combs, and owed me for all his board.

Since my residence at Haddam Neck, I have owned of boats, canoes and sail vessels, not less than twenty. These I mostly employed in the fishing and trafficking business, and in these occupations I have been cheated out of considerable money by people whom I traded with taking advantage of my ignorance of numbers.

About twelve years ago, I hired a whale boat and four black men, and proceeded to Long Island after a load of round clams. Having arrived there, I first purchased of James Webb, son of Orange Webb, six hundred and sixty clams, and afterwards, with the help of my men, finished loading my boat. The same evening, however, this Webb stole my boat and went in her to Connecticut river and sold her cargo for his own benefit. I thereupon pursued him, and at length recovered the boat, but for the proceed of her cargo I never could obtain any compensation.

Four years after I met with another loss, far superior to this in value, and I think by no less wicked means. Being going to New London with a grandchild, I took passage in an Indian's boat and went there with him. On our return, the Indian took on board two hogsheads of molasses, one of which belonged to Captain Elisha Hart, of Saybrook, to be delivered on his wharf. When we arrived there, and while I was gone, at the request of the Indian, to inform Captain Hart of his arrival and receive the freight for him, one hogshead of the molasses had been lost overboard by the people in attempting to land it on the wharf Although I was absent at the time and had no concern whatever in the business, as was known to a number of respectable witnesses, I was nevertheless prosecuted by this conscientious gentleman the Indian not being able to pay for it) and obliged to pay upwards of ten pounds lawful money, with all the costs of court. I applied to several gentlemen for counsel in this affair and they advised me, as my adversary was rich, and threatened to carry the matter from court to court till it would cost me more than the first damages would be,--to pay the sum and submit to the injury, which I accordingly did, and he has often since insultingly taunted me with my unmerited misfortune. Such a proceeding as this committed on a defenseless stranger almost worn out in the hard service of the world, without any foundation in reason or justice, whatever it may be called in a Christian land, would in my native country have been branded as a crime equal to highway robbery. But Captain Hart was a white gentleman, and I a poor African, therefore it was all right, and good enough for the black dog.

I am now sixty-nine years old. Though once straight and tall, measuring without shoes six feet, one inch and an half, and every way well proportioned, I am now bowed down with age and hardship. My strength, which was once equal if not superior to any man whom I have ever seen, is now enfeebled so that life is a burden, and it is with fatigue that I can walk a couple of miles, stooping over my staff. Other griefs are still behind, on account of which some aged people, at least, will pity me. My eye-sight has gradually failed, till I am almost blind, and whenever I go abroad one of my grandchildren must direct my way; besides for many years I have been much pained and troubled with an ulcer on one of my legs. But amidst all my griefs and pains, I have many consolations; Meg, the wife of my youth, whom I married for love and bought with my money, is still alive. My freedom is a privilege which nothing else can equal. Notwithstanding all the losses I have suffered by fire, by the injustice of knaves, by the cruelty and oppression of false-hearted friends, and the perfidy of my own countrymen whom I have assisted and redeemed from bondage, I am now possessed of more than one hundred acres of land, and three habitable dwelling houses. It gives me joy to think that I have and that I deserve so good a character, especially for truth and integrity.[1] (While I am now looking to the grave as my home, my joy for this world would be full--IF my children, Cuff for whom I paid two hundred dollars when a boy, and Solomon who was born soon after I purchased his mother--If Cuff and Solomon--Oh! that they had walked in the way of their father. But a father's

---

[1] *Note, the closing words in parenthesis were omitted in the later editions. It is probable that both improved later, especially so in the case of Solomon, who is well spoken of by elderly men now living, as having maintained a good character.*

lips are closed in silence and in grief!--Vanity of vanities, all is vanity.)

CERTIFICATE.

STONINGTON, CONN., November 3, 1798.

THESE may certify, that VENTURE is a free negro man, aged about 69 years, and was, as we have ever understood, a native of Africa, and formerly a slave to Mr. James Mumford, of Fisher's Island, in the State of New York, who sold him to Mr. Thomas Stanton, 2d, of Stonington, in the State of Connecticut, and said Stanton sold said VENTURE to Col. Oliver Smith, of the aforesaid place. That said VENTURE hath sustained the character of a faithful servant, and that of a temperate, honest and industrious man, and being ever intent of obtaining his freedom, he was indulged by his masters after the ordinary labor on the days of his servitude, to improve the nights in fishing and other employments to his own emolument, in which time he procured so much money as to purchase his freedom from his late master, Colonel Smith; after which he took upon himself the name of VENTURE SMITH, and has since his freedom purchased a negro woman, called Meg, to whom he was previously married, and also his children who were slaves, and said VENTURE has since removed himself and family to the town of East Haddam, in this State, where he hath purchased lands on which he hath built a house, and there taken up his abode.

NATHANIEL MINOR, ESQ.
ELIJAH PALMER, ESQ.
CAPT. AMOS PALMER.
ACORS SHEFFIELD.
EDWARD SMITH.

TRADITIONS OF VENTURE! KNOWN AS VENTURE SMITH.[2]
COMPILED BY
H. M. SELDEN.

SEVERAL editions of the Life of Venture have been published successively by his family, and by them circulated throughout the county, but more in the towns contiguous to his home, where the subject was well known for his abnormal strength, industry and goodly character, confirmatory of the

---

[2] Venture assumed the name of Smith in compliment to his latest master, Col. Oliver Smith, who generously permitted him to secure his freedom by his own earnings.

personal narrative. Copies of the remarkable autobiography were also sent by purchasers to friends abroad. It has long been out of print. To meet the demand for a new edition and to include traditions gathered by correspondence, personal intercourse with the aged and supplemented by some account of his family, is the object of the compiler. Tradition says Venture's amanuensis was Elisha Niles, of Chatham, who had been a school-teacher, and also a Revolutionary soldier, like one of the sons of Venture.

The reader of this new edition will find much in confirmation of the truthfulness of Venture's statements.

Among the different homes of Venture, the later and favorite one was in Haddam Neck, near the western shore of Salmon River, on higher ground and overlooking the cove. His farm was excellent land, fine mellow soil and very easy to till. In illustration of its fertility an old and current tradition says: "A black snake was once seen moving on and over the heads of the standing rye on one of the fields." His house was a one-story unpainted building, in the upper portion of which he had a room that he called his office. Here, after his decease, his younger son, Solomon, continued to live many years. A few rods from where it stood Wells C. Andrews built a large two-story house now owned by John H. Cone.

Venture presented a noble appearance. In mention of himself he says, "Though once straight and tall, measuring, without shoes, six feet one inch and a half, and every way well proportioned," etc. Tradition says he weighed over three hundred pounds and measured six feet around his waist. The tradition of the waist measure was received by the compiler from two sources. The first, from Mr. Orville Percival of Moodus, in 1894, then over 80 years of age, who said Venture measured six feet around his waist, that his feet were very large and twice the width of his (Mr. Percival's) father's feet.

The incident Venture relates of taking upon his knees a tierce of salt has with variation passed into tradition, or the act has been repeated. Mr. Percival gave it as occurring in a store at East Haddam, when Venture burst both of his brogan shoes in carrying the salt across the floor. Mr. Percival added: "A noted wrestler tried his skill in wrestling with Venture, but found he might as well try to remove a tree."

Mr. Alex, M. Clark of Haddam Neck, over 82 years of age, says that Venture worked occasionally for his grandfather, Robert Clark, and with his father, Benajah Clark, at the same time, and that he had often heard them say that Venture measured six feet around his waist, and one or both saw him measured; that Gersham Rowley, a brother of the late Eleazar Dunham Rowley of Young Street, Chatham, was present and assisted in the measurement. Mr. G. Rowley afterward moved to Farmersville, N. Y., where Mr. A. M. Clark visited and heard him relate the occurrence. Mr. A. M. Clark says he heard his father say that Venture weighed over 300 pounds; that his axe weighed nine pounds; that his usual day's work was seven cords of wood, but had cut nine cords in a day; that with his canoe he went often to Long Island, a distance of forty-five miles, to chop, and bring back clams on his return; that by his great strength he made the canoe go very straight and fast. Mr. Clark says that Venture called one day on his grandfather, Robert Clark, for him to stack some wheat, saying in disparagement of himself, "Nigger never know nothing!" Mr. Clark also related the tradition of the salt lifting and mentioned it as occurring in a store in East Haddam. Traditions vary sometimes.

Daniel Cone of Moodus gives the tradition of Venture's axe as weighing six pounds, and that he cut six cords of wood a day. He also repeated the salt-lifting tradition. Another tradition current over forty years ago was that Venture while chopping never raised his axe higher than his head, but forced it into the wood up to the eye at every blow, and further that he said he did not believe in chopping air. This appears to confirm the greater weight of his axe.

Mr. Robert S. Cone of Moodus writes: "About the weight of Venture's axe have no knowledge, but should think six pounds a light weight, for my father used a five and one-half pound weight." Mr. Cone adds: "I have heard father say that he and his brother Horatio cut wood for Venture at thirty-four cents per cord to pay for the use of his scow. When they went to get the scow she was well up on the beach. They thought it impossible to get her off. Venture said, 'Lead me down. True, I am blind, but I can give you a lift.' They led him to the water's edge. Father said the timbers fairly cracked as his great hands touched the scow. She swept into the water like a bird on the wing."

Another tradition, received from various sources, says that when Venture purchased oxen after his sight failed, his method of examining them, besides feeling, was to seize each ox by its hind legs and raise it up to estimate the weight. Again, that Venture while in the house of Ansel Brainerd, Sr., in Haddam Neck--who weighed two hundred or more--stooped down and, placing his hands palm upward on the floor, said to Mr. Brainerd, "You put your feet into my black paws and clasp your hands in my wool and I will raise you up!" This was done and Venture raised him up.

Among the early recollections of the compiler is his visiting an old, unoccupied gambrel-roofed house--the early home of his great-grandfather, Robert Chapman--having narrow outside doors. Tradition said that whenever Venture called, which he often did, he invariably turned sidewise to pass through.

Dea. E. C. Hungerford of Chester, in a letter of April 22, 1895, wrote: "The history of Venture will be interesting, I believe, to a great many. I shall want a copy, perhaps more than one.

"You ask me to rewrite my father's recollections of him. My father (born in 1777) told me that, when he was young, Venture often came to his father's house, and, as he was too heavy a burden to ride on a horse's back, he rode in a sort of two-wheeled cart. Sometimes his horse did not behave well, and then, Venture would put one hand in front of his horse's fore legs and one behind them and jounce the fore parts of the horse up and down a few times and remark, 'There!' The horse would usually behave well after such a jouncing. Father said he used to go behind Venture when he sat in an ordinary chair to look at his broad back and hips, which projected beyond the chair on each side, showing what a large man, he must have been."

There is a tradition that the owner of a valuable wood or timber lot, wishing to have some of it cut, had engaged Venture to do it. He arrived later than expected, for which the owner reproved him. Venture, displeased, replied, "You will have cut all you want." At noon the owner came, and to his great surprise and disgust found nearly the whole of his beautiful grove laid low. Robert S. Cone thinks the party whose wood Venture nearly demolished was Capt. Elisha Cone of East Haddam, as his home was Venture's headquarters when he was on that side of the river, but he must have been aware of

Venture's peculiarities. It is easy to suppose similar instances and in a different location.

Dr. A. B. Worthington of Middle Haddam, born in 1819, relate that tradition says Venture had engaged to cradle a field of grain. At noon he returned bearing the cradle, having finished the field, to the great surprise of the owner, who expected it would require more than a day to complete it.

Mrs. Philo Bevin of East Hampton, in her letter, of March 12, 1895, which we copy in full, gives a similar occurrence which, perhaps, may have originated the former:

EAST HAMPTON, CONN., March 12, 1895.

Mr. H. M. Selden:

DEAR SIR--I have been quite interested in the history of Venture, and my mother, who is living with me, at the age of 96 years and 9 months, is possibly the only living person in this vicinity who has personal recollections of him. Mother is the widow of Alfred I. Loomis of Westchester. Her maiden name was Abigail Foote, born in June, 1798, and in her childhood lived in S. W. district, known as Waterhole. Venture used to visit at a neighbor's, Mr. Bigelow, grandfather of D. S. Bigelow, who lives where his grandfather did when she was young. She says Venture froze his feet, and she remembers well that he walked on his knees and could travel quite fast, and for sport used to chase the children. She was afraid of him, and would never allow him to catch her, but Polly Bigelow would let him catch her. She says he was a very powerful men, and Mr. Bigelow one morning set him to cut down trees before breakfast and he hurried to call him away, fearing he would cut down the whole grove of timber. Perhaps you have heard all this, but I don't remember to have seen anything about his going on his knees, and possibly it may have been for only a little while. Mother is very bright and clear in her mind and her memory is better than the average of young folks, so I am sure she cannot be mistaken about this. I have promise of the loan of "Life of Venture" from a lady who lives here.

I don't suppose I have given you any points of interest, except to tell you there is one person living who remembers Venture, and I thought I would venture to write, peradventure it might add to your history.

Very respectfully yours,

MRS. PHILO BEVIN.

It is natural to suppose that the grove cutting on the Bigelow place was later than the one previously mentioned (thought to have been on the Capt. Elisha Cone farm), from the solicitude of the owner. The incident of the salt lifting related of Venture may have been reenacted by him (as mentioned in the tradition) on being appealed to by curious doubters. It is related of Venture that on the occasion of his marriage he threw a rope over the house of his master, where they were living, and had his wife go to the opposite side of the house and pull on the rope hanging there while he remained and pulled on his end of it. After both had tugged at it awhile in vain, he called her to his side of the house and by their united effort the rope was drawn over to themselves with case. He then explained the object lesson: "If we pull in life against each other we shall fail, but if we pull together we shall succeed." The success of his later life implies that the lesson was not forgotten by his true and loving wife.

At length, borne down with the weight of years and increasing infirmities, he sickened and died September 19, 1805, in his seventy-seventh year. His heavy body was conveyed in a boat across the Cove and carried thence on a bier, a distance of some three miles, to the cemetery adjoining the First Congregational Church in East Haddam, for burial, by four strong men fittingly chosen. The two in front were white, proving the respect he had won, while two of his own race assisted in the rear. Robert S. Cone writes of the pallbearers: "When Venture was buried, my father was one of the pallbearers. He was six feet three inches high. Uri Gates was six feet two inches high. Hannawell, a slave of Doctor Moseley, was five feet six inches high, and a slave of Gen. Epaphroditus Champion, about the same height, was his helper. The negroes being behind threw the weight upon themselves, and as they were mounting the long Olmsted hill the darkies complained bitterly. Hannawell exclaimed, 'Durned great nigger! Ought to have quartered him and gone four times. It makes the gravel stones crack under my feet.' "

His grave is marked by a brown-stone slab inscribed.

SACRED TO THE MEMORY
OF
VENTURE SMITH
AFRICAN.

Though the son of a King, he was kidnapped and sold as a slave, but by his industry he acquired money to purchase his freedom.

WHO DIED SEPT. 19, 1805,
IN YE 77TH YEAR OF HIS AGE.

A similar slab at the adjoining grave is inscribed:

SACRED TO THE MEMORY
OF MARGET SMITH,
RELICT OF VENTURE SMITH,
WHO DIED
DEC. THE 17TH, A. D. 1809,

A Narrative of the Life and Adventures of Venture

IN THE 79TH YEAR OF HER AGE.

CHILDREN OF VENTURE AND MARGRET SMITH.

Their names with supposed approximate dates of birth are gathered from the autobiography of their father.[3]

- 1. HANNAH, born about 1752. Her freedom was purchased for £44. She married a free negro named Isaac, and died --. No mention of children.
- 2. SOLOMON, born about 1756; died about 1773, in

---

[3] *Venture in the closing words of his autobiography disparages his sons Cuff and Solomon. The compiler, on inquiry among the elderly people who remembered them well, fails to find sufficient warrant for the language of criticism. Evidently, if any youthful foibles early appeared, they were soon overcome.*

his 17th year. His freedom was purchased for $200.

- 3. CUFF, born about 1758. His freedom was purchased for $200. Was a soldier in the Revolutionary War, credited to town of East Haddam, enlisted January 29, 1781, as a private for three years in Col. Heman Swift's Battalion. He married, but to whom is to the compiler unknown. Had seven children: 1st--Cuff; 2d--George; 3d--Daniel; 4th--Cynthia; 5th and 6th--twins, Jack and Alice; 7th--Venture, Jr., called Young Venture. Most of these were born in East Haddam. R. S. Cone thinks Cuff died in East Haddam. He was a very strong man, over six feet high. While he lived in Haddam Neck he worked some in the quarries and assisted in loading vessels from the quarries with his brother Solomon. While so engaged, they together alone carried aboard some very heavy stone, which on being unloaded in New York those assisting could not believe were carried aboard by two men alone. George, the second son of Cuff Smith, married and had several children, one of whom was Nelson of Haddam, the father of Charles, who was born in Haddam in 1847, and married Ascenath Hurd of East Haddam. They have eight children and reside in

Cobalt, worthy descendants of Venture.
- 4. SOLOMON, 2d, born 1773 or 1774, was a very strong man and over six feet high.

Mr. Robert S. Cone of Moodus, says: "Solomon had seven children. He was married twice. First, to Tamar, a worthy, useful woman. A friend to everybody, everyone her friend. Think she had two children. One, William, lived to grow to manhood, a straight, handsome fellow, well-formed and well spoken. Died in Hartford, unmarried.

"I recollect a short episode which occurred in my boyhood days in connection with the above William. We, that is, Tom

Summers with others and myself when a lad, were sailing up the Cove in a scow. Summers was tall and very conceited of his strength, thinking himself more than a match for the strong. Solomon's place was noted at that time for its early peaches, delicious apples and fine vegetables, far ahead of his neighbors. As we moved along, when the scow stood opposite Solomon's place, Summers remarked, 'Now for a bag of Sol's apples!" He jumped ashore, sprang up the hill into the orchard and began to gather. William soon appeared, tall, well dressed and very comely. He very politely asked Mr. Summers to go away. Instead, Mr. Summers showed his two fists in fighting array. William again said, 'Will you go? Will you go?' Summers still showed fight. William, with a cat-like movement, seized him by the nape of the neck and seat of his pants and tossed him down the bank to the Cove with as little effort as we would manage a little child.

"Solomon's second wife was as unlike. Tamar as possible. Her name was Peggy. She had six children. Hannah first; then two daughters Don't recollect their names.[4]

4th--Henry; 5th--Oliver; then Eliza, for many years head chamber-maid on the Hartford and New York line of boats, later on the largest of the Fall River

---

[4] Mary and Harriet.

line, the 'Puritan.' Solomon, the father, died in East Haddam at the home of George Palmer, where his daughter Eliza was brought up."

Mrs. L. E. Sexton of Turnerville write: "I well remember Solomon and his wife Peggy. They came often to the store at Rock. Landing kept by John L'Homedieu. One day she came alone and Mr. L'Homedieu kindly inquired after her husband, calling him Sol. (He was often called Sol Venture.) She repeat the name after him in anything but a pleased manner, saying, 'Why, Sol and Solomon are no more alike than Hagar and Phyllis," giving him a lecture for speaking of her husband in such a disrespectful manner.

"I remember Solomon as tall, straight and broad-shouldered, but I think she carried her head quite as high as he did. I think only two of their children attended school on Haddam Neck--two boys, one named George Oliver Washington Smith. The other one had a name equally as long, but I only remember one of them, Henry. The winter that Azariah Wheeler taught the school they attended and were his pet class He had them come and stand by the table. First, he would drill them to get the right kind of bow, then each one had to give his name in full. By that time the whole school was interested, but if any smiled too broadly he would try to look severe and rap on the table with his ruler to call the house to order, but I think he enjoyed the fun with them and was quite willing the school should, too. He was a good teachers and helped to make all the children happy, and that is half the battle whether at school or at home."

The compiler remembers both Solomon and George Oliver W. Smith. The former as being tall and straight, the latter a very bright young man, who married, lived in Middletown and died there several years since, leaving children.

It is related of Solomon that, calling at Capt. Justin Sexton's while he and his boys were engaged in butchering, he quoted the words, "Where the carcass is, there the eagles will be gathered together," and added, "among them comes a black crow and begs a piece of liver." He received some liver. There is a tradition that a large colored family called at Solomon's home early one morning, to remain through the day. They were unwelcomed by Mrs. Peggy; who did not wish a visitation. She placed a small pot inside a larger one and both over the fire. Noon came, long passed, and night succeeded in turn; the pot boiled without ceasing and the hungry visitors at length withdrew. The father remarked later, that for all he knew the "pawt" was still boiling.

Several have claimed, or been claimed by others, as

descendants of Venture. Yet the omission of their names from his autobiography casts doubt upon their claims. Among these was Diana, or Dinah Caples, more generally called 'Dian, and remembered by the elderly people. She often boasted of being a grand-daughter to the king. She made and sold baskets and artificial birds. Of the latter she feared some might learn the manufacture. In person she was of unusual proportions, about five feet in height and nearly as broad.

Robert S. Cone writes: "Tradition says Gideon Quash was Venture's son. He was near the age of Cuff. Both were Revolutionary soldiers. Gid, so said, resembled Venture in form, speech and feature. He was by far the most intelligent negro for miles; accumulated thousands of dollars; married a white wife whom he told me he obtained her consent to become his, by himself showering into her lap a bag containing ninety-six hard dollars, one year's pay from government. His descendants still live in Colchester, owners of property and respected."

Dr. A. B. Worthington says that Quash called at Isham's store in Colchester and wanted to purchase a "book-tionary and a diction," for his son Jim to learn the meaning of words. Jim later showed his ability by teaching in Colchester.

Alex. M. Clark says, "Sanford, who lived with Solomon, was a son of Solomon's first wife previous to her marriage with Solomon, and that he attended school in Haddam Neck and lived with the family."

www.ingramcontent.com/pod-product-compliance
Lightning Source LLC
Chambersburg PA
CBHW080545090426
42734CB00016B/3204